SUPER SIMPLE
PET
CRITTER CRAFTS

Fun and Easy Animal Crafts

Alex Kuskowski

Consulting Editor, Diane Craig, M.A./Reading Specialist

Super Sandcastle

An Imprint of Abdo Publishing
abdopublishing.com

abdopublishing.com

Published by Abdo Publishing, a division of ABDO, PO Box 398166, Minneapolis, Minnesota 55439. Copyright © 2017 by Abdo Consulting Group, Inc. International copyrights reserved in all countries. No part of this book may be reproduced in any form without written permission from the publisher. Super SandCastle™ is a trademark and logo of Abdo Publishing.

Printed in the United States of America, North Mankato, Minnesota
062016
092016

THIS BOOK CONTAINS
RECYCLED MATERIALS

Editor: Liz Salzmann
Content Developer: Nancy Tuminelly
Craft Production: Frankie Tuminelly
Cover and Interior Design and Production: Colleen Dolphin, Mighty Media, Inc.
Photo Credits: Mighty Media, Inc.; Shutterstock
The following manufacturers/names appearing in this book are trademarks:
Crayola®, Paper Mate®, Sharpie®

Library of Congress Cataloging-in-Publication Data
Names: Kuskowski, Alex, author.
Title: Super simple pet critter crafts : fun and easy animal crafts / by Alex
   Kuskowski ; consulting editor, Diane Craig, M.A./reading specialist.
Description: Minneapolis, Minnesota : Abdo Publishing, [2017] | Series: Super
   simple critter crafts
Identifiers: LCCN 2016000307 (print) | LCCN 2016001998 (ebook) | ISBN
   9781680781632 (print) | ISBN 9781680776065 (ebook)
Subjects: LCSH: Handicraft--Juvenile literature. | Pets--Juvenile literature.
Classification: LCC TT160 .K87437 2017 (print) | LCC TT160 (ebook) | DDC
   745.59--dc23
LC record available at http://lccn.loc.gov/2016000307

TO ADULT HELPERS

The craft projects in this series are fun and simple. There are just a few things to remember to keep kids safe. Some projects require the use of sharp or hot objects. Also, kids may be using messy materials such as glue or paint. Make sure they protect their clothes and work surfaces. Review the projects before starting, and be ready to assist when necessary.

. . . .

KEY SYMBOL

Watch for this warning symbol in this book. Here is what it means.

 HOT!
You will be working with something hot. Get help from an adult!

Super SandCastle™ books are created by a team of professional educators, reading specialists, and content developers around five essential components—phonemic awareness, phonics, vocabulary, text comprehension, and fluency—to assist young readers as they develop reading skills and strategies and increase their general knowledge. All books are written, reviewed, and leveled for guided reading and early reading intervention programs for use in shared, guided, and independent reading and writing activities to support a balanced approach to literacy instruction.

CONTENTS

PERFECT PETS

We love our pets! They make great friends. They are fun to play with and teach.

We can learn from our pets too. People who have pets learn responsibility. Pets give love and companionship to the people who care for them.

Show your love for your pets! Make some fun crafts all about your pet. Or make crafts of a pet you want to have.

GET TO KNOW YOUR PET!

Fun FACTS ABOUT some POPULAR PETS

FISH

Betta fish are a common type of pet fish. They come in many colors and patterns.

DOGS

More people own a pet dog than any other animal. There are more than 100 different dog breeds.

Snakes

Snakes use their tongues to smell. That's how they track their prey.

BIRDS

There are more than 9,000 bird **species**. **Parakeets**, **finches**, and **cockatiels** are common pet birds.

SPIDERS

A common spider to have as a pet is a **tarantula**. They can regrow lost legs.

CATS

Cats don't meow at other cats. They only meow at humans. It's how they get our attention.

HAMSTERS

Hamsters are active pets. They can run 1 mile (1.6 km) a day!

LIZARDS

Bearded dragons are common pet lizards. They can grow up to 2 feet (61 cm) long!

UNITED KINGDOM

Many people in the United Kingdom love pet fish. Ten percent of homes there have them.

WORLD PETS

PEOPLE EVERYWHERE LIKE TO HAVE PETS! LEARN ABOUT THE MOST POPULAR PETS AROUND THE WORLD.

EGYPT

Ancient Egyptians worshipped cats. They called them "mau."

CHINA

Keeping pet crickets started in ancient China. Now people all over the world have pet crickets!

TAIWAN

Tortoises are **symbols** of long life in Taiwan. A tortoise can live longer than 50 years.

JAPAN

Japan has many cat cafés. People at these cafés can play with cats while eating and drinking.

9

MATERIALS

HERE ARE SOME OF THE THINGS YOU'LL NEED TO DO THE PROJECTS.

acrylic paint

air-dry clay

chenille stems

clear flat marbles

clear plastic
snow globe

craft feathers

felt

fishing line

foam brushes

googly eyes

hot glue gun
& glue sticks

paintbrushes

paper

paper fasteners

permanent
marker

picture frame

pom-poms

raffia

round paper
lantern

tagboard

tissue paper

wire

KITTY CAT FRAME

THIS FRAME WILL MAKE ANY PICTURE "MEOW-VALOUS"!

MATERIALS

newspaper	small paintbrush	craft glue
picture frame	tagboard	3 chenille stems
acrylic paint, 2 colors	scissors	pencil
foam brush		

1 Cover your work surface with newspaper. Take the glass and backing out of the frame. Use the foam brush to paint the front of the frame one color. Let the paint dry. Add a second coat if needed.

2 Use the small paintbrush to paint stripes on the frame with the other color. Make them look like a cat's stripes. Let the paint dry.

3 Cut two triangles out of tagboard. These are the cat's ears. Glue the ears to the top of the frame. Let the glue dry.

4 Cut the chenille stems in half. These are the **whiskers**. Wrap a whisker around a pencil and then remove it. Curl a second whisker the same way.

5 Glue one curly and two straight whiskers to each side of the frame. Let the glue dry.

6 Choose a photo to put in your cat frame.

FLOATING LANTERN FISH

TURN YOUR ROOM
INTO a FISH TANK!

MATERIALS 🔥

white & black paper
scissors
craft glue

round paper lantern,
   8–10 inches
   (20–25 cm)
gold tissue paper

ruler
hot glue gun
   & glue sticks
fishing line

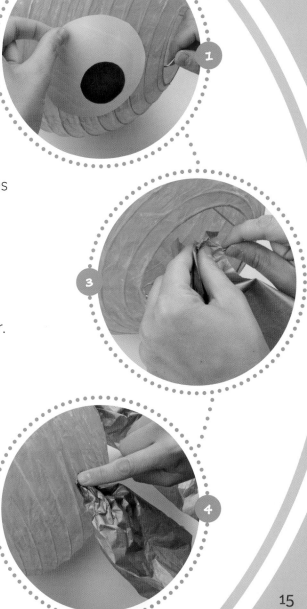

1. Cut two circles out of white paper. Cut two circles out of black paper. Make the black circles smaller than the white circles. Glue the black circles to the white circles. These are the fish's eyes. Glue the eyes to the lantern. Place them near the small opening.

2. Cut a 10-inch (25 cm) square out of tissue paper. Cut two rectangles out of tissue paper. Make them each 4 by 12 inches (10 by 30 cm).

3. Gather one side of the tissue-paper square together. Hot glue it to the wire in the large lantern opening. This is the fish's tail.

4. Fold one tissue-paper rectangle in half crosswise. Pinch the folded end together. Hot glue it to one side of the lantern. Fold and glue the other rectangle to the other side of the lantern. These are the fish's fins.

5. Cut a long piece of fishing line. Tie one end to the wire on each end of the lantern. Use the line to hang up your fish!

LITTLE HAMSTER BALL

make a cute hamster in a cozy home!

MATERIALS

clear plastic snow globe	scissors	large brown pom-pom
tan raffia	craft glue	2 googly eyes
ruler	small pink bead	brown felt

1. Take the cap off the snow globe. Cut about 100 ½-inch (1.3 cm) pieces of raffia. Put them in the snow globe.

2. Glue the pink bead to the brown pom-pom. This is the hamster's nose. Glue the googly eyes above the bead.

3. Cut two rounded ears out of felt. Glue them above the eyes.

4. Glue the bottom of the pom-pom to the inside of the snow globe cap. Let the glue dry.

5. Carefully put the cap on the globe. Turn the globe right-side up.

17

POLKA-DOT COILED SNAKES

CURL UP WITH THESE cute snakes!

MATERIALS

newspaper	paper plate	2 googly eyes
acrylic paint	pencil with eraser	craft glue
paintbrush	scissors	red paper
toilet paper tube		

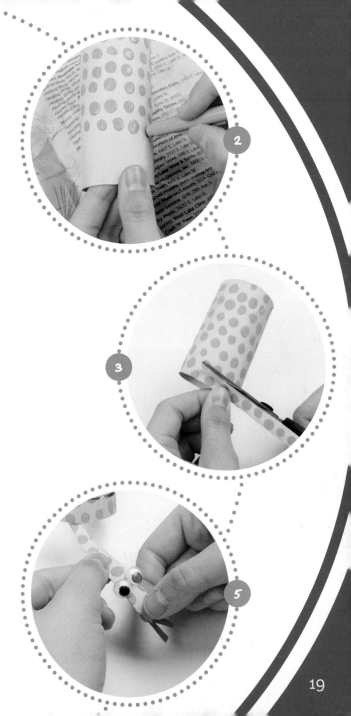

1. Cover your work surface with newspaper. Paint the inside and outside of the tube. Let the paint dry.

2. Put a small amount of another color of paint on the paper plate. Dip the pencil's eraser in the paint. Make rows of dots around the tube. Let the paint dry.

3. Cut the tube into a **coil**. Start at an angle at one end of the tube. Cut the tube into a long strip.

4. Glue the googly eyes near one end of the strip.

5. Cut a V shape out of red paper for the snake's tongue. Glue the tongue under the end with eyes.

6. Repeat steps 1 through 5 to make your snake some friends!

CREEPY CRAWLY SPIDER

make a crawler for your room!

MATERIALS 🔥

newspaper

clear flat marble

black & white acrylic
   paint

foam brush

small paintbrush

permanent marker

wire

scissors

ruler

hot glue gun
   & glue sticks

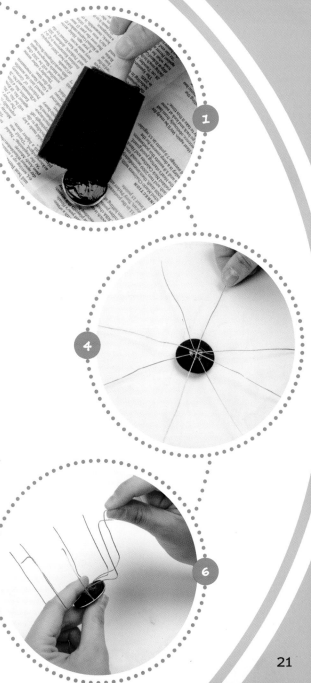

1 Cover your work surface with newspaper. Paint the bottom of the marble black. Let the paint dry.

2 Dip the small paintbrush in white paint. Paint two white dots on the top of the marble. These are the eyes. Let the paint dry.

3 Use a permanent marker to add a small black dot in each eye.

4 Cut four pieces of wire. Make each piece 6 inches (15 cm) long. Put hot glue in the center of the bottom of the marble. Lay the wires over the glue. Cross them in the middle so they are evenly spaced. Let the glue dry.

5 Measure 1 inch (2.5 cm) out from the edge of the marble along a wire. Bend the wire down. Repeat with the other wires.

6 Bend about ¼ inch (0.6 cm) of each wire out at the bottom. Now your spider has legs it can stand on!

21

FUZZY LIZARD FRIENDS

MAKE FRIENDLY GECKOS THAT REALLY STAND OUT!

chenille stems, various   ruler   craft glue
   colors   scissors   googly eyes
pencil

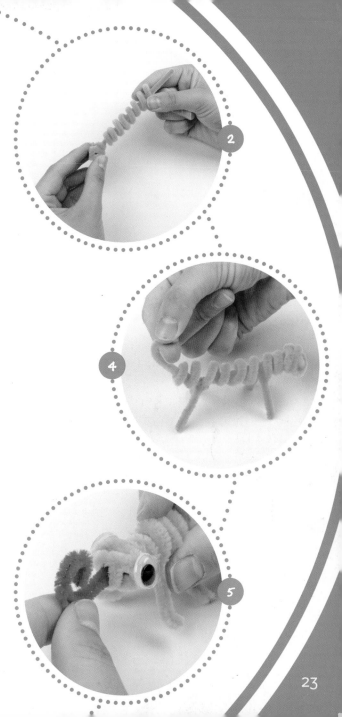

1   Choose three chenille stems of the same color. Fold one stem in half. Make a small **loop** at the fold. Wrap one end of the chenille stem around the loop. This is the head.

2   Wrap a second chenille stem around the pencil. Take it off the pencil. Slide it over the straight end of the first chenille stem. This is the body.

3   Cut two 3-inch (7.5 cm) pieces off the third chenille stem. Wrap the middle of one piece around the straight stem near the head. Wrap the other piece around the straight stem near the end of the body. These are the legs. Bend the ends to make feet.

4   Curl the end of the straight stem to make a tail. Glue a googly eye to each side of the head.

5   Cut a 2-inch (5 cm) piece of a second color of chenille stem. Curl one end. Stick the other end into the head. This is the tongue.

6   Repeat steps 1 through 5 to make more geckos.

HIGH-FLYING PARROT

make a
COLORFUL
BIRD
TO Hang
anyWHERE!

MATERIALS

chenille stems, various colors

ruler

scissors

small pom-poms

large pom-pom

craft glue

googly eyes

craft feathers

suction cup hooks

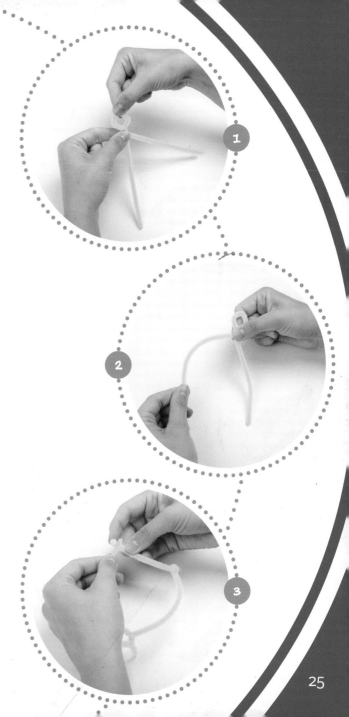

1 Decide what color to make the parrot's swing. Choose three chenille stems of that color. Bend one of them in half. Twist the center to make a small circle.

2 Bend the sides of the chenille stem so they curve.

3 Cut a 3-inch (7.5 cm) piece off the second chenille stem. Twist one end of this shorter piece and one end of the first chenille stem together. Do the same with the other ends.

4 Cut the third stem and the rest of the second stem into 2-inch (5 cm) pieces.

(continued on next page)

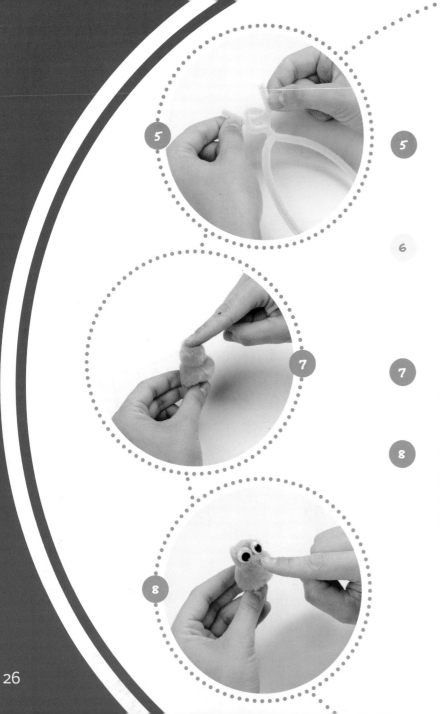

5. Put one short piece through the **loop** in the first chenille stem. Twist the ends together to make another small loop.

6. Put another short piece through the loop you just made. Twist the ends together. Repeat until all the short pieces are used. The swing is complete.

7. Choose a small and a large pom-pom of the same color. Glue them together to form the parrot's head and body.

8. Glue two googly eyes to the small pom-pom. Cut a ¼-inch (0.5 cm) piece of orange chenille stem. Glue it under the googly eyes for the beak.

9 Choose a chenille stem for the wings. Cut two 2-inch (5 cm) pieces off the stem. Bend them into teardrop shapes. Glue a teardrop shape to each side of the large pom-pom.

10 Cut a 3-inch (7.5 cm) piece of orange chenille stem. Bend it in half. Glue the fold to the bottom of the large pom-pom. This makes the legs.

11 Glue the bottom of the bird to the inside of the swing, on the straight edge. Bend the legs around the swing.

12 Glue three feathers to the back of the bird above the legs.

13 Put the top **loop** of the swing on the suction cup hook. Use it to hang your parrot on a mirror or window!

CLAY PUPPY PAL

make a dog that can be your new pal!

MATERIALS

air-dry clay	paintbrush	2 colors of felt
sewing needle	permanent marker	scissors
water	2 googly eyes	paper fastener
gray acrylic paint	craft glue	

1 Roll a ball of clay. Bend it into a **kidney bean** shape. This is the dog's body.

2 Roll another ball of clay that is smaller than the first one. Shape it into an oval. This is the head.

3 Use the needle to scratch crisscross lines on the body where the head will go. Do the same on the head where it will connect to the body. Be careful when using the needle. It is very sharp.

(continued on next page)

4 Dip your finger in water. Dab the water on the marked areas of both clay pieces. Press the head onto the body gently but firmly. Let the clay dry according to the directions on the package.

5 Paint spots on the head and body. Let the paint dry.

6 Draw a nose and mouth on the dog with permanent marker.

7 Glue the googly eyes to the head. Let the glue dry.

8   Choose a color of felt for the ears and tail. Cut out two small floppy ear shapes. Glue them behind the eyes.

9   Cut out a tail shape. Glue it to the back end of the body.

10 Choose a color of felt for the collar. Cut a strip out of the felt. Make sure it is long enough to wrap around the dog's neck.

11 Push a paper fastener through the center of the collar. Fold the ends of the fastener flat along the back of the collar. This is the collar's tag.

12 Wrap the collar around the dog's neck. The paper fastener should be in front. Glue the ends in place. Cut off any extra felt.

GLOSSARY

cockatiel – a small gray parrot with a yellow head.

coil – a spiral or a series of loops.

finch – one of many kinds of songbirds that eat seeds and grains.

kidney bean – an edible seed that is usually dark red.

loop – a circle made by something such as yarn, string, or wire.

parakeet – a small parrot with brightly colored feathers and a long, pointed tail.

species – a group of related living beings.

symbol – something that stands for something else.

tarantula – a type of large hairy spider that can bite but isn't very harmful to people.

whisker – one of the long hairs around the mouth of an animal.